Persian (Farsi & Dari) Phrasebook with Transliteration

Yavar Dehghani

Introduction

Language is more than a tool for communication. It is a window into how people see the world.

This Persian (Farsi & Dari) Phrasebook with Transliteration invites you to explore not only the words and expressions used across Iran and Afghanistan, but also the shared spirit of hospitality, poetry, and connection that defines Persian culture.

Persian (known as Farsi in Iran and Dari in Afghanistan) belongs to the Indo-Iranian branch of the Indo-European family. Despite its beautiful script and rich literary history, spoken Persian is straightforward and melodic, making it surprisingly easy for learners to pick up. Even a few words or phrases, spoken with sincerity will open doors and hearts across Persian-speaking communities.

This phrasebook has been designed for learners, travelers, and anyone who wishes to engage meaningfully with Persian speakers. Each section introduces practical expressions for daily life — from greetings and directions to social customs, shopping, and food. The transliteration system allows you to pronounce Persian words accurately even if you are unfamiliar with the Persian script.

The book also provides concise grammar explanations, cultural insights, and examples from both Farsi and Dari, making it a bridge between two major variants of Persian. You will notice that the Dari forms appear in bold, highlighting where pronunciation or usage differs.

What to Expect in This Book

•	Essential phrases for travel, conversation, and everyday interaction

•	Side-by-side English, Persian, and transliteration for quick learning

•	Grammar and pronunciation guides that simplify structure and sound

•	Cultural notes that help you understand the nuances of politeness, hospitality, and social etiquette

•	Practical sections covering topics such as food, transport, accommodation, emergencies, and more

Whether you are travelling through Iran or Afghanistan, connecting with Persian-speaking friends, or studying the language formally, this phrasebook will serve as your reliable companion—a key to communication, and a bridge to understanding.

Abbreviations Used in This Chapter

adj   adjective

n   noun

pol   polite

pl   plural

sg   singular

PRONOUNCIATION

The pronunciation of Persian is easy and straightforward. Unlike in English, there is a consistency between pronunciation and spelling. Stress is generally on the last syllable of the word as in ketäbkhäne 'li-brary'. However, the stress on proper names is on the first syllable as in khashäyär.

VOWELS

The vowel system in Persian is simple and consists of six vowels. The first back vowel (ä, u, o) in the word becomes long, as in ääsän 'easy' or estefääde 'benefit'. These vowels are:

a   as the 'a' in 'ask' and 'fast'

e   as the 'e' in 'get' and 'fell'

i   as the 'i' in 'fit' and 'pitch'

o   as the 'a' in 'ball' or the 'o' in 'mole'

u   as the 'u' in 'rule' and 'push'

ä   as the 'o' in 'top' or 'a' in 'father'

CONSONANTS

Most Persian consonants are pronounced like their English counterparts. The consonants, which are pronounced similar to the English ones, are listed here:

b as the 'b' in 'boy'

ch as the 'ch' in 'cheese'

d as the 'd' in 'door'

f as the 'f' in 'feet'

j as the 'j' in 'jar'

m as the 'm' in 'me'

n as the 'n' in 'net'

s as the 's' in 'sin'

sh as the 'sh' in 'she'

t as the 't' in 'toy'

v as the 'v' in 'vest'

y as the 'y' in 'yes'

z as the 'z' in 'zip'

There are three consonants in Persian, which do not exist in English. These consonants are:

kh as the 'ch' in the Scottish 'loch'. It is pronounced at the back of the mouth, when the root of tongue makes smooth contact with the end of the palate.

gh, a guttural sound like a heavy French 'r', which is also pronounced at the back of the mouth, when the root of tongue makes a sudden contact with the end of the palate

zh. As the 'zh' in 'Zhivago' or the 'g' in 'mirage'

' A glottal stop which is pronounced in the throat and marks a break in the flow of speech.

The following consonants are slightly different from their English counterparts:

l Persian l is pronounced in the front of the mouth, so it is similar to the 'l' in 'life', but not the 'l' in 'role'

k It is similar to the English 'k' before and after 'ä, u, o' but it is palatalized
with 'i, e, a' which is similar to the 'ck' in 'backyard'
g like 'k' has two forms: it is like the 'g' in 'got' before or after 'ä, o, u', and
similar to the 'g' in 'get' before or after 'a, e, i'
r similar to a trilled 'r' in English but never silent or diphthongized.
h as in the 'h' in 'hit'. It is never silent.
All Persian consonants can be doubled where they are always pronounced
distinctly as in 'hot tea' but not in 'kettle'

TRANSLITERATION

The transliteration system in this phrasebook tries to teach you the
pronunciation of the formal style of Persian, which can be used in all Persian
speaking countries. For ease of learning, only the Farsi examples are used in
the grammar section.

This phrasebook is useful for Farsi and Dari speaking places. The main
emphasis is on Farsi. However, the Dari equivalents have been provided in
bold when necessary.

GRAMMAR

Persian is an inflectional language, that is, the verb is conjugated for person
and number of the subject. So, unlike in English, the subject can be omitted
from the sentence, as in this example.

I went home. man be madrase raftam   be madrase raftam
            (lit: I-to school went-I)   (lit: to school went-I)

The language system is much easier and more regular than English to learn and remember. This section will try to provide a simple and basic grammar of Persian, although it cannot cover all aspects of the grammar in these few pages. The transliteration of the examples in this chapter is in written style.

WORD ORDER

The basic word order in Persian is subject, object, and verb, which is different from English. However, this order is not fixed especially in the spoken style where the verb can come before the object. Because the verb is conjugated for the subject, the subject can usually be omitted from the sentence. Thus, even if you cannot remember the word order, Persian speakers will understand you, no matter where in the sentence you tell the verb.

ARTICLES

Persian has different means to express articles like 'the' and 'a/an'. The word ye 'one' before the noun or the sound i after the noun conveys the meaning of the English article 'a/an'. For example:

I saw a boy in the street.   pesari rä dar khiyäbän didam

                                    (lit: boy-a in the street saw-I)

Otherwise, the noun is definite, as in:

I saw the musuem. man muze rä didam.

                    (lit: I museum saw-I)

NOUNS

Nouns in Persian do not have gender. They are pluralized by adding hä to the end of the noun, as in:

book   ketäb

books   ketäbhä

car   mäshin

cars   mäshinhä

However, unlike in English, nouns in Persian do not pluralize when they
come after numbers more than one, as in:

'one house'   yek khäne

'two houses'   do khäne

'ten houses'   dah khäne

There are only a few irregular nouns borrowed from Arabic like eyd 'festival'
a'yäd 'festivals'.

Noun cases

Noun cases in Persian are marked by a preposition or postposition. Each case
shows the role of the noun in the sentence as a subject or object. There are six
noun cases in Persian.

Nominative case

The subject in the sentence always has a nominative case and it does not take
any preposition or postposition, like utubus 'bus' in:

The bus left.   utubus raft

                                     (lit: the bus went-it)

Accusative case

 This case shows that the noun is the direct object of the sentence. It is formed
by the postposition rä, which comes after the noun, as in:

I saw Shiraz.   man shiräz rä didam

                       (lit: I Shiraz saw-I)

Dative case

This case is formed by adding the preposition be to the noun and indicates
that the noun is an indirect object, as in:

I went to Tehran.   man be tehrän raftam

                           (lit: I to Tehran went-I)

Locative case

This case shows the location where an action takes place. It is formed by
adding the preposition dar to the noun, as in:

Can I meet you in the hotel?   mitavänam shomä rä dar hotel beb-inam?

                           (lit: can-I you in the hotel see-I)

Ablative case

This case indicates the origin of an action. It is formed by adding the
preposition az to the noun, as in:

I came from Tabriz today. man emruz az tabriz ämadam.

                           (lit: I today from Tabriz came-I)

Pronouns

Because all Persian verbs are conjugated for person and number of the
subject, the subject pronouns, like nouns, can be omitted from the sentence.
In the phrasebook, we have put the subject pronouns inside parenthesis to
show that they are optional. Unlike in English, the second person in Persian
has two forms: to for the singular and shomä for the plural. In Modern
Persian, the plural form is also used for the singular for politeness. to is only
used among close friends and relatives. The third person singular has only
one form, än:

I	man	we	mä
you	to	you(pl)	shomä
he/she/it	än	they	änhä

There are suffixed personal pronouns equivalent to each of the above
pronouns. These pronouns are affixed to the end of a noun to show the
possession. For example, ketäb am 'my book', ketäb at 'your book'.

my	am	our	emän
your	at	your(pl)	etän
his/her/its	ash	their	eshän

VERBS

Verbs in Persian are conjugated for the person and number of the sub-ject as
well as for tense. Therefore, by adding the fixed set of suffixes to the verb
root, you can easily make all forms of a verb. The verb root in Persian is
formed by deleting the suffix dan from the infinitive. For ex-ample, the
infinitive form for the verb 'to read' is khändan and its verb root is khänd. To
form the past tense, we can simply add the past tense suffixes to this root:

| I read. | khändam |
| We read. | khändim |

Present tense

The present tense is formed by the prefix mi before the verb and adding the
personal suffixes am, i, ad, im, id, and to the end of the verb, as in these
examples:

I read.	mikhänam	We read.	mikhänim
You read.	mikhäni	You read(pl).	mikhänid
He/she reads.	mikhänad	They read.	mikhänand

Past Tense

Past tense is formed by adding the personal suffixes dam, di, d, dim, did, dand to the verb root, as in these examples:

I read.	khändam	We read.	khändim
You read.	khändi	You(pl) read	khän-did
He/she/it reads.	khänd	They read.	khändand

To form the continuous past tense, you can just add the prefix –mi to these forms, as in mikhändam 'I was reading'.

Future Tense

The future tense seems complicated for foreign visitors, but it has a systematic and regular structure. To form the future, the verb root khäh 'want' is conjugated with the personal suffixes, and comes before the main verb, which always is in the past tense form for the third person singular. For example, khäham khänd (lit: want-I read) 'I will read' is formed by adding am to khah 'want' which is followed by the past tense of khan 'read', as in these examples:

I will read.	khäham khänd
You will read.	khähi khänd
He/she will read.	khähad khänd
We will read.	khähim khänd
You (pl) will read.	khähid khänd
They will read.	khähand khänd

In colloquial speech, the present form can also be used for future with-in the context, as in: fardä mikhänam (lit: tomorrow read-I) 'I will read tomorrow'.

Imperative

The imperative form of a verb is formed by adding the prefix be to the verb root, as in: bekhor 'Eat!' and bekhän 'Read!'. The negative form of the imperative is formed by adding na to the beginning of the verb root, as in:

Don't eat!   nakhor!

Don't read!   nakhän!

TO BE   budan

The verb 'to be' is irregular in Persian. In the present tense, its form is e 'is' and in the past tense bud 'was'. However, like other verbs it is conjugated by adding personal suffixes. This verb can be added to nouns, adjectives, or adverbs. For example, teshne plus eam means 'I am thirsty."

I am thirsty.   teshne eam

You are thirsty.   teshne ei

He/she/it is thirsty.   teshne e

We are thirsty.   teshne eim

You(pl) are thirsty.   teshne eid

They are thirsty.   teshne eand

In colloquial speech, e can be omitted (except for the third person singular). For example, teshne am (lit: thirsty-I) 'I am thirsty'.

Compound verbs

In Persian, there are many compound verbs which are formed by a noun or an adjective followed by a simple verb form like kardan 'to do', shodan 'to become', and raftan 'to go', which is conjugated for tense and person/number. In modern Persian, the number of these compound verbs is increasing. Some examples are as follows:

I cried.   gerye kardam

	(lit: cry did-I)
I destroyed.	kharäb kardam
	(lit: destroed did-I)
I climbed.	bälä raftam
	(lit: up went-I)
I stood up.	boland shodam
	(lit: long became-I)

Adjectives

Adjectives in Persian, unlike in English, come after the noun. They do not agree in number with the noun they modify, so they always have the same form, as in:

| good book | ketäb e khub |
| good books | ketäbha ye khub |

Only superlative adjectives come before the noun. Comparative adjectives are formed by adding tar, and superlatives are formed by adding tarin to the end of the adjective, as in:

the pretty house	khäne ye zibä
the prettier house	khäne ye zibätar
the prettiest house	zibätarin khäne

Possession

Possession in Persian is shown by using the vowel e, which is called 'Ezafe' and conveys possession and ownership. This vowel is inserted between the noun and the following word, which describes or qualifies it, as in:

| my book | ketäb e man |
| your house | khäne ye shomä |

'Ezafe' takes the form of ye when the noun ends in a vowel.

your ticket	belit e shomä
the city center	markaz e shahr

QUESTIONS

Questions in Persian are formed by a rise in intonation at the end of the sentence. So, unlike in English, there is no change in word order, as in:

The plane is leaving.	haväpeymä harekat mikonad.
	(lit: plane move did-it)
The plane is leaving?	haväpeymä harekat mikonad?

In the written style, the word äyä is added to the start of the sentence but in the spoken style it is not used.

The plane is leaving?	äyä haväpeymä harekat mikonad?
	(lit: does plane move do-it)

Question words

Where	kojä
Why	cherä
When	key
what	che
how	chetor
who	ki
which	kodäm

Where is the bank?

bänk kojäst?

Why is the museum closed?

cherä muze baste ast?

When does the festival begin?

jashn key shuru' mitavänin?

What is he saying?

u che migoyad?

How do I go there?

chetor änjä beravam?

Who is she?

u ki e?

Which is the best?

kodäm behtar ast?

Negatives

To form the negative in a sentence, the prefix na is placed before the verb, as in:

He went to Tehran.   u be tehrän raft

                                (lit: he to Tehran went-he)

He did not go to Tehran.   u be tehrän naraft

For the future tense, na is added to the first verb, as in:

He will go to Tehran.   u be tehrän khähad raft

                                (he to Tehran want-he went)

He will not go to Tehran.   u be tehrän nakhahad naraft

Key Verbs

Regular verbs

The following verbs are regular, and most Persian verbs are conjugated like them.

khändan (to read)

	Present	Past	Continuous past	Future
I	mikhänam	khändam	mikhändam	khäham khänd
you	mikhäni	khändi	mikhändi	khähi khänd
he/she/it	mikhänad	khänd	mikhänd	khähad khänd
we	mikhänim	khändim	mikhändim	khähim khänd
you (pl)	mikhänid	khändid	mikhändid	khähid khänd
they	mikhänand	khändand	mikhändand	khähand khänd

khordan (to eat)

	Present	Past	Continuous past	Future
I	mikhoram	khordam	mikhordam	khäham khord
you	mikhori	khordi	mikhordi	khähi khord
he/she/it	mikhorad	khord	mikhord	khähad khord
we	mikhorim	khordim	mikhordim	khähim khord
you (pl)	mikhorid	khordid	mikhordid	khähid khord
they	mikhorand	khordand	mikhordand	khähand khord

kharidan (to buy)

	Present	Past	Continuous past	Future
I	mikharam	kharidam	mikharidam	khäham kharid
you	mikhari	kharidi	mikharidi	kähi kharid
he/she/it	mikharad	kharid	mikharid	khähad kharid
we	mikharim	kharidim	mikharidim	khähim kharid
you (pl)	mikharid	kharidid	mikharidid	khähid kharid
they	mikharand	kharidand	mikharidand	khähand kharid

ävardan (to bring)

	Present	Past	Continuous past	Future

	Present	Past	Continuous past	Future
I	miyävaram	ävardam	miyävardam	khäham ävard
you	miyävari	ävardi	miyävardi	khähi ävard
he/she/it	miyävarad	ävard	miyävard	khähad ävard
we	miyävarim	ävardim	miyävardim	khähim ävard
you (pl)	miyävarid	ävardid	miyävardid	khähid ävard
they	miyävarand	ävardand	miyävardand	khähand ävard

Useful irregular verbs

budan (to be)

	Present	Past	Continuous past	Future
I	eam	budam	mibudam	khäham bud
you	ei	budi	mibudi	khähi bud
he/she/it	e	bud	mibud	khähad bud
we	eim	budim	mibudim	khähim bud
you (pl)	eid	budid	mibudid	khähid bud
they	eand	budand	mibudand	khähand bud

raftan (to go)

	Present	Past	Continuous past	Future
I	miravam	raftam	miraftam	khäham raft
you	miravi	rafti	mirafti	khähi raft
he/she/it	miravad	raft	miraft	khähad raft
we	miravim	raftim	miraftim	khähim raft
you (pl)	miravid	raftid	miraftid	khähid raft
they	miravand	raftand	miraftand	khähand raft

däshtan (to have)

	Present	Past	Continuous past	Future

	Present	Past	Continuous past	Future
I	däram	däshtam	midäshtam	khäham däsht
you	däri	däshti	midäshti	khähi däsht
he/she/it	därad	däsht	midäsht	khähad däsht
we	därim	däshtim	midäshtim	khähim däsht
you (pl)	därid	däshtid	midäshtid	khähid däsht
they	därand	däshtand	midäshtand	khähand däsht

tavänestan (to be able to)

	Present	Past	Continuous past	Future
I	mitavänam	tavänestam	mitavänestam	khäham tavänest
you	mitaväni	tavänesti	mitavänesti	khähi tavänest
he/she/it	mitavänad	tavänest	mitavänest	khähad tavänest
we	mitavänim	tavänestim	mitavänestim	khähim tavänest
you (pl)	mitavänid	tavänestid	mitavänestid	khähid tavänest
they	mitänand	tavänestand	mitavänestand	khähand tavänest

dädan (to give)

	Present	Past	Continuous past	Future
I	midäham	dädam	midädam	khäham däd
you	midähi	dädi	midädi	khähi däd
he/she/it	midähad	däd	midäd	khähad däd
we	midähim	dädim	midädim	khähim däd
you (pl)	midähid	dädid	midädid	khähid däd
they	midähand	dädand	midädand	khähand däd

dänestan (to know)

	Present	Past	Continuous past	Future
I	midänam	dänestam	midänestam	khäham dänest

	Present	Past	Continuous past	Future
you	midäni	dänesti	midänesti	khähi dänest
he/she/it	midänad	dänest	midänest	khähad dänest
we	midänim	dänestim	midänestim	khähim dänest
you (pl)	midänid	dänestid	midänestid	khähid dänest
they	midänand	dänestand	midänestand	khähand dänest

kardan (to do)

	Present	Past	Continuous past	Future
I	mikonam	kardam	mikardam	khäham kard
you	mikoni	kardi	mikardi	khähi kard
he/she/it	mikonad	kard	mikard	khähad kard
we	mikonim	kardim	mikardim	khähim kard
You (pl)	mikonid	kardid	mikardid	khähid kard
they	mikonand	kardand	mikardand	khähand kard

khästan (to want)

	Present	Past	Continuous past	Future
I	mikhäham	khästam	mikhästam	khäham khäst
you	mikhähi	khästi	mikhästi	khähi khäst
he/she/it	mikhähad	khäst	mikhäst	khähad khäst
we	mikhähim	khästim	mikhästim	khähim khäst
you (pl)	mikhähid	khästid	mikhästid	khähid khäst
they	mikhähand	khästand	mikhästand	khähand khäst

MEETING PEOPLE

Persians are kind and hospitable especially towards foreigners. Knowing a few Persian formal words for thanking them and saying goodbye will help a lot.

YOU SHOULD KNOW

Hello.

saläm

Goodbye.

khodä häfez/be amäne khodä

Yes.

bale

No.

na/ney

Excuse me.

bebakhshid

Please.

lotfan

Thank you.

motashakkeram/tashakkur

Many thanks.

kheyli mamnun

OK.

bäshe

Do you mind?

eshkäl nadärad?

That's OK

khähesh mikonam/mehrabäni

GREETINGS & GOODBYES

Verbal greetings in Persian are usually accompanied by hand shaking and sometimes kissing on the cheek. Both take place only be-tween people of the same sex. Thus, people do not shake or kiss on the cheek with the opposite sex in greetings, unless they are close families, e.g. brother and sister. Greetings with the opposite sex are just verbal and more formal than with the same sex. Kissing on the cheek usually takes place between friends and relatives who have not seen each other for a long time.

Good morning.

sob bekheyr

Good day (noon).

ruz bekheyr

Good afternoon.

asr bekheyr

Good evening.

shab bekheyr

Hello/Hi.

saläm

Goodbye.

khodä häfez

CIVILITIES

People say saläm 'hello' to a friend or relative who is approaching them. If they have got time, they stop and ask about each other's health: häletän chetor e? (jurin?) They do not call each other by their first name unless they add äghä (sähib) 'Mr' or khänom 'Mrs' before the name. People are usually called by their surname, and only chil-dren are called by the first name. Close friends also call each other by first name.

Thank you very much.

kheyli motashakkeram/tashakkur

You're welcome.

khahesh mikonam /mehrabäni

Excuse me/Sorry. (pol)

ma'zerat mikhäham

May I/Do you mind?

eshkäl nadärad?

How are you?

 häletän chetor e/jurin?

Fine!

khobam

Not bad!

bad nistam

You have gone to a lot of trouble.

 kheyli zahmat keshidin/khayli be zahmat shodin

Let's go.

befarmäyin beravin.

Please sit down

befarmäyin beshinin

Correct!

Doroste/sahih ast

That will do.

käfiye

Do you understand?

motavajjeh mishavid/mifahmin?

Yes, I understand.

bale mifahmam

No, I don't understand.

na namifahmam

Please wait a while

lotfan kami sabr konin

FIRST ENCOUNTERS

Persians are very hospitable and kind towards foreigners and even after a short conversation may invite you to their home.

How are you?

häletän chetor e/jurin?

Fine. And you?

khobam. shomä chetor eid/shumä jur astin?

What is your name?

esmetän chi e/nämetän chi e?

My name is ... .

esm/näm am… hast.

I'd like to introduce you to ...

mikhäham shomä rä be … mo'arefi konam.

I'm pleased to meet you.

az äshnäyitän khoshbakhtam.

I'm a friend of Farid.

man dust Faridam.

His/her name is … .

esm/näm esh …. hast

MAKING CONVERSATION

Do you live here?

shomä injä zendegi mikonid?

Where are you going?

shomä kojä miravid?

What are you doing?

shomä chikär mikonid/che mikonid?

What do you think about ...?

shomä dar mored …chi fekr mikonid?

Can I take a photo of you?

mitavänam akse shomä rä begiram

What is this called?

esm/näm e in chi e?

Beautiful, isn't it!

ghashange, mage na/maghbul hast.nist?

It's very nice here.

injä kheyli khub hast.

We love it here.

mä injä rä dust därim/mä injä rä khosh därim.

What a cute baby!

che bachche ye ghashangi/che tifl maghbuli!

Are you waiting too?

shomä ham montazer in?

That's strange!

ajibe!

That's funny (amusing)

khandedar hast

Are you here on holiday?

shomä baräye ta'tilät/rukhsati injä ämadin?

I'm here ... .

man ... injä hastm.

for a holiday

baräye ta'tilät/rukhsati

on business

baräye tejärat

to study

baräye tahsil

How long are you here for?

cheghadr injä mimänin?

I'm here for .... weeks/days.

män ... hafte/ruz injä mimänam

Do you like it here?

az injä khoshetän miyäd /injä rä khosh därin?

We like it here very much.

mä az injä kheyli khoshemän miyäd /mä injä rä khayli khosh därim

Where are you staying?

shomä kojä mimänin?

How long have you been here?

shomä che moddat hast ke injä hastin?

I've been here three days.

man se ruz hast ke inja hastm.

This is my first visit to Iran.

in avvalin mosäferat e man be iran hast

Are you here on your own?

shomä injä tanhä hastid?

I'm here with my friend

man injä bä dust am hastam.

Thanks. I don't smoke.

motashakkeram. man sigär nemikesham/ man segret nemikesham.

I will call you later.

man ba'dan be shomä zang mizanam.

USEFUL PHRASES

Sure.

hatman.

Just a minute.

yek daghighe sabr konin.

It's OK.

eyb nadärad.

It's important.

mohemm hast.

It's not important.

mohemm nist.

It's possible.

emkän därad.

It's not possible.

emkän nadärad.

Look!

negäh konin

Listen/Listen to this!

gush konin/ba in gush konin.

I'm ready.

man ämäde am

Are you ready?

shomä ämäde in?

Good luck!

movaffagh bäshin.

Just a second!

yek lahze shabr konin!

NATIONALITIES

Where are you from?

shomä kojäyi hastid?

I'm from ... .

man ahl e ... am.

Australia

ostäräliyä /ästaräliyä

Austria

otrish /ästeriyä

Canada

känädä

England

ingilis /inghiland

Europe

urupä /yurup

Germany

älmän /jarmani

India

hend/hindustän

Ireland

Irland/äyrland

Japan

zhapon /japan

Spain

Espäniyä/ispayn

Sweden

su'ed /suwidin

the USA

ämrikä

I come from ... .

man az … miyäyam.

I live in ... .

man dar … zendegi mikonam.

the city

shahr

the countryside

rustä/gharya

the mountains

kuhestän

CULTURAL DIFFERENCES

How do you do this in your country?

shomä dar keshvaretän in rä chetor anjäm midahid?

Is this a local or national custom?

in yek rasm e mahali hast yä melli?

I don't want to offend you.

man nemikhäham be shomä bi-ehterämi bekonam.

I'm sorry, it's not the custom in my country.

mota'ssefam, in dar keshvar e man rasm nist.

I'm not accustomed to this.

man be in kär ädat nadäram.

In my country, we …

dar keshvar e man, mä …

My culture/religion does not allow me to …

farhang/mazhab e man be man ejäze nemidahad …

do this

in kär rä bekonam

drink/eat this

in rä bekhoram

AGE

How old are you.?

shomä chand säletän hast?

I'm … years old.

man … säl am hast

How old do you think I am?.

fekr mikonid chand säl am hast?

I think you are … years old.

fekr mikonam shomä … säletän hast

How old is your son/daughter

pesar/dokhtar e shomä chand sälesh hast?

He/she is … years old.

un … sälesh hast

OCCUPATION

Where do you work?

kojä kär mikonid?

What (work) do you do?

chi kar mikonid?

I am a/an … .

man … am

artist

honarmand/artist

businessperson

täjer

doctor

doctor/däktar

engineer

mohandes/injinar

factory worker

kärgar/gharibkär

farmer

keshävarz/dehghän

journalist

ruznäme negär/journalist

lawyer

vakil

mechanic

mekänik /mekhanik

nurse

parastär/nars

office worker

kärmand

scientist

däneshmand

secretery

monshi/sakratar

student

däneshju/muta'alim

teacher

mo'allem

waiter

ghärson

writer

nevisande

I'm … .

man … am

unemployed

bikär

retired

bäzneshaste/mutaghä'id

I'm self-employed.

man shoghl e äzäd däram

Do you like your job?

shoghletän rä dustdärin?

/wazifatän rä khosh därin?

What are you studying?

shomä chi mikhänin?

I'm studying … .

man … mikhänam

art

honar

arts/humanities

ulum e ensäni

business

bäzargäni/tijärat

engineering

mohandesi/injinari

languages

zabän/lisän

law

hughugh

medicine

pezeshki/tibb

Persian

färsi

science

ulum

teaching

dabiri/tadris

RELIGION

What is your religion?

mazhab e shomä chi hast?

I am (a) … .

man … am

Buddist

budäyi

Catholic

kätolik

Christian

Masihi/isawi

Hindo

hendu

Jewish

yahudi/juhud

Muslem

mosalmän

I'm not religious.

man mazhabi nistam

I believe in God.

man be khodä e'teghäd däram

FEELINGS

I'm ... .

man ... am

angry

asabäni

happy

khoshhäl/khosh

hungry

gorosne

thirsty

teshne

tired

kaste/mända

Are you ...?

shomä ... hastid?

sad

närähat/parishän

sleepy

khäbälud

sorry (condolence)

Worried

negaran

Are you hot?

shomä garm etän hast?

Are you in a hurry?

shomä ajale därin?

LANGUAGE DIFFICULTIES

Do you speak English?

shomä ingilisi baladin/yäd därin?

Yes, I do.

bale, baladam/yäd däram

No, I don't.

na, balad nistam/yäd nadäram

Does anyone speak English here?

injä kasi ingilisi balad hast/yäd därad)?

I speak a little.

man ye kami balad am/yäd däram

Do you understand?

motavajjeh mishavid?

I (don't) understand.

(na) mifahman

Could you speak more slowly?

mitavänin yaväsh/ähista tar sohbat konin/gap bezanin?

Could you repeat that?

mitavänin uno tekrär konin?

How do you say ...?

 … rä chetori miguyin?

What does ... mean?

ma'ni ye … chi hast?

What languages do you speak?

che zabänhäyi baladin? /che lisänhäyi yäd därin?

I speak English and German.

man ingilisi va älmäni baladam   /man ingilisi va jerman yäd däram

I don't speak Persian

man färsi balad nistam/yäd nadäram

Do you have an interpreter?

shomä motarjem/tajumän därin?

GETTING AROUND

Finding Your Way

Where is the ...?

 ... kojä ast?

bus station

terminal/istayshin

train station

istgah e ghatär/istayshine rayl

the city centre

markaz e shahr

the bus stop

istgäh e utubus /istayshine bas

Excuse me, can you help me please?

bebakhshin, mitvänin lotfan be man komak konin?

I'm looking for … .

man donbäl e … migardam

How do I get to …?

chetor mitavänam be … beravam?

Is it far from here?

än az injä dur hast?

Where are we now?

mä hälä kojä hastim?

What's the best way to get there?

behtarin räh e raftan be änjä kodäm hast?

Can I walk there?

man mitavänam piyäde be änjä beravam?

Can you show me on the map?

mitavanin dar naghshe be man neshän bedahid?

What time does the … leave/arrive?

 … che sä'ati harekat mikonad/miresad?

aeroplane

haväpeymä/tayyära

boat

ghäyegh /kashti

bus

outbus/bas

train

ghatär/rayl

What … is this?

in kodäm … hast?

street

khiyäbän/sarak

city

shahr

village

deh/gharya

Directions
Turn …
Bepichin/dor bekhorin …
at the traffic lights

sare cherägh / dar ishära

at the roundabout

däkhele meydän / girdiye tirafiki

To the right.

samte räst

To the left.

samte chap

You can go on foot.

mitavänin piyäde beravin

go straight ahead.

mostaghim beravin.

behind

aghab

in front of

jeloye

far

dur

near

nazdik

opposite

moghäbel

here

injä

there

änjä

north

shomäl

south

junub

east

shargh

west

gharb

BUYING TICKET

Where can I buy a ticket?

kojä mitavänam belit/tikat bekharam?

We want to go to …

mä mikhähim be … beravin

Do I need to book?

läzem hast ke rezerv konam?

I'd like to book a seat to …

man yek jä baräye …mikhäham

It is full.

por hast

I'd like …

man …mikhäham

a one-way ticket

yek belite yek sare /yak tikate yak tara

a return ticket

yek belite do sare /yak tikate do tara-fa

two tickets

do tä belit/do tikat

a student's fare

yek belite däneshjuyi/

yak tikate muta'allimi

a child's fare

yek belite bachche/yak tikate tifl

1st class

dareje yek

2nd class

dareje do

I require a … meal.

man ghazä ye … mikhäham

hot

garm

with meat

goshti

I'd like to … my ticket

mikhäham belit/tikat am rä … bekonam

cancel

kansel

change

avaz

confirm

känfirm

How long does this trip take?

in mosäferat cheghadr tul mikeshad?

I'd like a window seat.

man yek sandali kenäre panjeremikhäham/ man yak choki kenäre kelkin mi-

khäham

AIR

Is there a flight to Esfahän tonight?

emshab be Esfahän parväzi därin?

Is this a nonstop flight?

in parväz bedune tavaghghof hast?

What is the flight number?

shomäre/namber e parväz chand hast?

Can I go to the airport by bus?

mitavänam bä utubus be furudgäh beravam?

/mitavänam bä bas be maydäne haväyi beravam?

When is the next flight to Shiraz?

parväz e ba'di be shiräz key hast?

How long does this flight take?

in parväz cheghadr tul mikeshad?

What time do I have to be at the airport?

che sä'ati bäyad dar furudgäh/maydäne hawäyi bäsham ?

Where is the baggage claim?

ghesmat e tahvil e vasäyel/sämän kojä hast?

I'd like to check in my luggage.

mikhäham bär am rä tahvil bedam

What's the charge for each excess kilo?

har kilo ezäfe bär chand hast?

My luggage hasn't arrived

bär e man nareside

AIRPORT TAX
avärez e furudgäh /
mäliyaye maydäne hawäyi

arrivals

vurud

departure

harekat

domestic

däkheli

exchange

ta'viz

flight

parväz

gate

dar e khuruji

international

beynolmelali

passport

gozarnäme/päsport

plane

haväpeymä /tayyära

transit lounge

salon e teräns

AT CUSOMS

I have nothing to declare.

man chizi baräye ezhär kardan nadäram

I have something to declare.

man chizi baräye ezhär kardan däram

Do I have to declare this?

man bäyad in rä ezhär konam?

This is all my luggage.

koll e bär e man in hast

May I go through?

mitavänam rad beshavam?

I didn't know I had to declare it.

man nemidänestam ke bäyad in rä ezhär konam

May I call my embassy/consulate?

mitavänan be sefärat/konsulgari am telefon konam?

BUS & COACH

Where is the bus stop?

istgäh e utubus kojä hast?/ istayshen e bas kojä hast?

Which bus goes to ...?

kodäm utubus/bas be … miravad?

Do you stop at ...?

shomä dar … tavaghghof därin?

Two tickets, please

lotfan, do tä belit/tikat

Does this bus go to ...?

in utubus/bas be … miravad?

How often do buses come?

 utubus/bas key be key miyäyad?

What time is the ... bus?

 utubus/bas e … key miyäd?

next

ba'di

first

avval

last

äkhar

Could you let me know when we get to ...?

mitavänin vaghti be … residim be man beguyin?

Where do I get the bus for ...?

man kojä mitavänam utubus/bas e … rä savär shavam?

I want to get off.

man mikhäham piyäde shavam

TAXI

Is this taxi free?

in täksi khäli hast?

Please take me to ...

lotfan man rä bebarin be ...

this address

in ädres

the airport

furudgäh/maydäne hawäyi

the city centre

markaz e shahr

the railway station

istghäh e räh ähan /estashene rayl

How much is the fare?

keräye che ghadr hast?

Do you get extra for luggage?

baräye bär pul e ezäfi migirin?

Are you going to…?

shomä be…miravid?

Please don't take any other passengers.

lotfan mosäfer e dige savär nakonin

How much do I owe you?

che ghadr bäyad be shomä bedaham?

Instructions

Continue!

edäme bedahid!

The next street to the left/right.

khiyäbän e ba'di bepichin samt e chap/räst

/sarak e ba'di dawr bekhorin samt e chap/räst

Please slow down.

loftan yaväsh/ähista beravin

Please wait here.

lotfan injä montazer bäshin

Stop here!

injä negah därin

Stop at the corner.

in kenär negah därin

ACCOMMODATION

FINDING ACCOMMODATION

I'm looking for a ...

man donbäl e yek ... migardam

cheap hotel

hotel e arzän

clean hotel

hotel e tamiz

nearby hotel

hotel e nazdik

Where is the ... hotel?

...hotel kojä hast?

best

behtarin

cheapest

arzäntarin

What is the address?

ädresesh kojä hast?

Could you write the address, please?

mitavänin lotfan ädres rä benevisin?

BOOKING AHEAD

I'd like to book a room.

mikhäham yek otägh rezerv konam

Do you have a vacant room?

otägh khäli därin?

For (three) nights.

baräye (se) shab

How much for ...?

baräye … cheghadr mishavad?

one night

yek shab

a week

yek hafte

two people

do nafar

We will be arriving at ...

mä … miresim

My name is ...

esm/näm e man … hast

Is there hot water all the time?

äb e garm hamishe hast?

I'm not sure how long I'm staying.

motma'n nistam cheghadr mimänam

We'll be staying for two weeks.

mä do hafte mimänim

CHECKING IN

Do you have any rooms available?

otägh khäli därin?

Sorry, we're full.

mota'assefäne jä nadärim

Do you have a room with two beds?

otägh e dokhäbe därin?

Do you have a room with a double bed?

otägh e dotakhte därin?

I'd like …

man…mikhäham

a shared room

yek otägh e moshtarek

a single room

yek otägh e taki

We want a room with a …

mä yek otägh bä yek…mikhähim

bathroom

dastshuyi/tashnäb

shower

dush/shawer

TV

televiziyon

window

panjere/kelkin

Can I see it?

man mitavänam än rä bebinam?

Are there any other rooms?

otäghä ye digar ham hast?

Are there any cheaper rooms?

otäghä ye arzäntari ham hast?

Do you charge for the baby?

baräye nozäd ham keräye migirin?

can I pay by credit card

mitavänam bä kiridit kard bepardäzam

Do you require a deposit?

bey'äne ham mikhähin?

How many Toman?

chand toman?

Where is the manager?

modir kojä hast?

Where is the bathroom?

dastshuyi/tashnäb kojä hast?

Is there hot water all day?

äb e garm hamishe hast?

How much for ...?

baräye...cheghadr mishavad?

one night

yek shab

a week

yek hafte

two people

do nafar

Is there a discount for chil-dren/student

baräye bachchehä/däshjuhä (at-fäl/muta'alimin) takhfifi hast?

It's fine. I'll take it.

khobe. man än rä mikhäham

AROUND TOWN

Where is the ...?

 ... kojä hast?

bank

bänk

consulate

konsulgari

embassy

sefärat

post office

edäre ye post

public telephone

telefon e umumi

public toilet

tuvälet e umumi/tashnäb e umumi

town square

meydän e shahr

cinema

sinemä

hotel

hotel

market

bäzär

museum

muze /miyuziyum

police

polis

tourist information office

edäre ye jahängardi

MAKING A CALL

Hello, is ... there?

alo, … änjä hast?

Hello. (answering a call)

alo/bale

May I speak to ...?

mitavänam bä … sohbat konam/

gap bezanam?

Who's calling?

shomä ki hastin?

It's ....

man … am

Yes, he/she is here.

bale än injä äst

One moment, (please).

yek daghighe (lotfan)

I'm sorry, he's not here.

mota'ssefam, än injä nist

What time will she be back?

un key barmigarde?

Can I leave a message?

mitavänam yek peyghäm bezäram/bemänam?

Please tell her I called.

lotfan behesh beguyin man zang zadam

I'll call back later.

ba'dan zang mizanam

SIGHTSEEING

Where is the tourist office?

edäre ye jahängardi kojä hast?

Do you have a local map?

shomä naghshe ye mahalli därin?

What are the main attraction?

mahal hä ye didani kojähä hastand?

I'd like to see ...

man mikhäham ... rä bebinam

What time does it open?

än key bäz mishavad?

What time does it close?

än key baste mishavad?

What is that building?

än säkhtemän/ta'mir chiy hast?

What is this monument?

in äsäre bästäni chi hast?

How old is it?

än cheghadr omr däre?

May we take photographs?

mitavänim aks begirim?

Could you take a photograph of me?

mitavänin yek aks az man begirin?

Can we come inside?

mitavänim däkhel biyäyim?

Do you need an admission charge?

shomä vurudi ham migirin?

Is there a discount for…

takhfifi baräye…hast?

children

bachchehä/atfäl

students

däneshjuhä/muta'alimin

castle

ghal'e

church/cathedral

kelisä

cinema

sinemä

concert

konsert

crowded

shulugh/birobär

park

pärk

statue

mojassame

university

däneshgäh/pohantun

GOING OUT

Where to go

Do you want to go…?

mikhähin be…beravin?

How much does it cost to get in?

vurudi ye än cheghadr hast?

It's free of charge.

än majjäni hast?

I like to go to…

man mikhäham be…beravam

a cafe

yek ghahve khäne

a restaurant

yek resturän

the theatre

te'ätr

It's beautiful here.

injä ghashang/maghbul hast

I had a good time.

be man kheyli khosh gozasht

ARRANGING TO MEET

At what time shall we meet?

key hamdigar rä bebinim?

Where shall we meet?

kojä hamdigar rä bebinim?

Let's meet at eight o'clock.

sä'at e hasht hamdigar rä bebinim

OK. See you then.

bäshe.pas ba'dan shomä rä mibinam

Sorry, I am late.

bebakhshin, man dir kardam

Never mind!

eyb nadärad!

FAMILY

Are you married?

shomä mota'ahhel in?

Are you engaged?

shomä nämzad därin?

How many children do you have?

shomä chand tä bachche/tefl därin?

How many brothers/sisters do you have?

chand tä khähar/barädar därin?

I'm…

man…am

single

mojarrad

married

mota'ahhel

engaged

nämzad

I'm divorced.

man talägh gerefte am

How many children do you have?

shomä chand tä bachche/tefl därin?

How old is your child?

bachche/tefl tän chand säl däre?

Does he/she attend school?

un madrese/maktab miravad?

I don't have any children?

man bachche/tefl nadäram

I have a daughter/a son.

man yek dokhtar/yek pesar däram

I live with my family.

man bä khäneväde am zendegi mikonam

baby

nozäd

child

bachche/tefl

dad

bäbä/bäbi

daughter

dokhtar

father

pedar

father-in-law (husband's father)

pedar shohar/khosur

father-in-law (wife's father)

pedar zan/khosur

girl

dokhtar

gradfather

pedar bozorg/pedar kalan

grandmother

mädar bozorg/mädar kalan

husband

shohar

mother-in-law (husband's mother)

mädar shohar/khushu

mother-in-law (wife's mother)

mädar zan/khushu

mother

mädar

sister

khähar

son

pesar/bachcha

wife

zan

SHOPPING

Where can I buy ...?

man kojä mitavänam … bekharam?

Where is the nearest ...?

nazdiktarin … kojä hast?

barber

äräyeshgäh/salmäni

bookshop

ketäb furushi

camera shop

durbin furushi/kamerä furushi

chemist/pharmacy

därukhäne/daväkhäna

clothing store

lebäs furushi/kälä furushi

general store

furushgäh/dukän

dry cleaner

khoshk shuyi

market

bäzär

souvenir shop

kädo furushi/tohfa furushi

newsagency

ruznäme furushi/akhbär furushi

optician

eynak furushi

shoe shop

kafsh furushi/but furushi

stationers

laväzem ottahrir/ghirtäsiya

travel agency

äzhäns e mosäferati

I'd like to buy ...

man mikhäham … bekharam

Do you have others?

shomä chizhä ye digar ham därin?

I don't like it.

man az än khosh am nemiyäd

/man än rä khosh nadäram

Can I look at it?

mitavänam be än negäh konam?

I'm just looking.

man faghat negäh mikonam

How much is this?

in chand hast?

I'll buy it.

man än rä mikharam

Please wrap it.

lotfan baste bandi konin

Can I have a receipt?

mitavänin resid bedahid?

I'd like to return this.

man mikhäham in rä pas bedaham

It's faulty.

kharäb hast

It's broken.

shekaste hast

Can you give my money back.

mitavänin pul am rä pas bedahid?

I think it's too expensive.

fekr mikonam kheyli gerän/gheymat hast

It's too much for us.

baräye mä kheyli hast

Can you lower the price?

mitavänin nerkh rä kamtar konin?

Its price is very high.

nerkhesh kheyli bälä/boland hast

Do you have something cheaper?

shomä chiz e arzäntar ham därin?

I don't have much money.

man pul e ziyädi nadäram

I'll give you 2000 Toman

man 2000 toman be shomä midaham

Give me…

… be man bedahid

a kilogram

yek kilogeram

a liter

yek litr

half

nesf

I'd like …

man …mikhäham

battery

bätri

bread

nän/nän e khoshk

butter

kare/maska

cheese

panir

chocolate

shokolät

egg

tokhm e morgh/tokhum

flour

ärd

honey

asal

margarine

märgärin

matches

kebrit/gogard

meat

gusht

milk

shir

pepper

felfel/murch

salt

namak

shampoo

shämpo

soap

säbun

sugar

shekar/bura

toilet paper

käghaz tuvälet

toothpaste

khamir dandän/kerim e dandän

yoghurt

mäst

SOUVENIRES

basket

sabad

brassware

vasäyel e berenji

handicraft

sanäye' e dasti

miniature

miniyätor

rug

farsh/ghalin

pottery

vasäyel e sofäli/geli

jewllery

javäherät

silverware

vasäyel e noghreyi

Fretwork

monabbat käri

jacket

kot/jäkat

jumper (sweater)

poliver/jämpar

pants

shalvär/patlon

shirt

pirhan

shoes

kafsh/but

socks

juräb

swimsuit

mäyo

T-shirt

tishert

underwear

lebäs e zir

clothes

lebäs/kälä

boots

putin/chakme

coat

pälto/bälä push

dress

pirähan e zanäne

jeans

jin

pantyhouse

juräb shalväri

stockings

juräb e zanäne

umberrla

chatr

Can I try it on?

mitavänam emtähän esh bekonam?

My size is…

säyz e man … hast

It does not fit.

andäze nist

It's too…

kheyli…hast

big

bozorg/kalän

small

kuchik/khurd

short

kutäh

long

boland

tight

tang

loose

goshad

MATERIALS

Metal

felezzi

of brass

berenji

of gold

talä

ceramic

serämik

cotton

katän

hand made

dast säz

glass

shishe

leather

charm

of silver

noghreyi

plastic

pelästiki

silk

abrishami

sainless steel

istil

synthetic

masno'i

wool

pashmi

wood

chubi

COLOURS

dark ...

... tire

light ...

... roshan

black

siyäh

blue

äbi

brown

ghahveyi/naswäri

green

sabz

purple

banafsh/arghaväni

red

ghermez/sorkh

white

sefid

yellow

zard

orange

närenji

pink

surati/goläbi

grey

khäkestari

TOILETRIES

comb

shäne/boras

dental floss

nakh e dandän

deodorant

zedd e aragh

hair brush

bores

razor

rishtaräsh

razor blade

tigh

sanitary napkins

navär behdäshti

shampoo

shämpu

shaving cream

khamir rish

soap

säbun

sissors

gheychi

sunblock

kerem e zedd e äftäb

tissues

dastmäl käghazi

toilet paper

käghaz tuvälet

toothbrush

mesväk/bräsh

toothpaste

khamir dandän/kirime dandän

SMOKING

A packet of cigarettes, please.

lotfan ye baste sigär/segret

Are these cigarettes strong or mild?

in sigär/segret ghavi hast yä moläyem?

Do you have a lighter/matches?

shomä fandak/läyter/kebrit/gogard därin?

Do you mind if I smoke?

eshkäl nadärad man sigär/segret bekesham?

Please don't smoke.

lotfan sigär/segret nakeshin?

Would you like a cigarette

shomä sigär/segret mikhähin?

I'm trying to give up.

man sa'y mikonam tark konam

cigarettes

sigär/segret

filtered

filterdär

lighter

fandak/läyter

matches

kebrit/gogard

pipe

pip

tobacco

tanbäku

SIZES & COMPARISONS

small

kuchik/khurd

big

bozorg/kalan

heavy

sangin/gerang

light

sabok

more

ziyäd

little (amount)

too much/many

keyli ziyäd

many

kheyli

enough

käfi

also

ham

a little bit

yek kam

kam

FOOD

breakfast

sobhäne/näne sobh

lunch

nähär/näne chasht

supper

asräne

dinner

sham/näne shab

VEGETERIAN & SPECIAL MEALS

I'm a vegetarian.

man sabzikhär am

I don't eat meat.

man gusht nemikhoram

I don't eat chicken or fish.

man morgh yä mähi nemikhoram

I can't eat dairy products.

man nemitavänam labaniyyät bekhora

Do you have any vegetarian dishes?

shomä ghazähäye sbazikhäri därin?

Does this dish have meat?

in ghazä gusht därad?

Can I get this without meat?

mitavänam bedune gusht begiram?

Does it contain eggs?

tokhm e morgh därad?

I'm allergic to (peanuts).

be (bädäm zamini) hassäsiyat däram

Is this organic?

in tabi'i hast?

EATING OUT

Table for (five), please.

miz baräye (panj nafar) lotfan

May we see the menu?

mitavänim menu rä bebinim?

I'd like lunch.

man nähär mikhäham

What do you recommend?

shomä chi pishnehäd mikonid?

What's this dish?

in ghazä chi hast?

I'd like something to drink.

man nushidani mikhäham

Please bring me some ...

lotfän baräye man kami ... biyävarin

salt

namak

water

 äb

pepper

felfel/murch

bread

nän/näne khoshk

drink

nushäbe

an ashtray

zirsigäri

the bill

surat hesäb

a fork

changäl/panja

a glass of water

yek livän äb

(with/without ice)

(bä/bedun e yakh)

a knife

chäghu

a plate

boshghäb

cup

fenjän

sweet

shirin

fresh

täze

spicy

tond

AT THE MARKET

Meat & poultry

beef

gusht e gäv

chicken

morgh

goat

gusht e boz

heart

del

kedney

gholve/gurda

lamb

gusht e gusfand

liver

jegar

meat

gusht

quail

belderchin

tongue

zabän

turkey

bughalamun/filmorgh

veal

gusht e gusäle

Fish & Seafood

ancovies

mähi ye koli

fish

mähi

caviar

khäviyär

trout

ghezel älä

prawns

meygu

sardin

särdin

tuna

ton e mäh

VEGETABLES

beans

lubiyä

cabbage

kalam/karam

carrot

havij/zardak

cauliflower

gol e kalam/gholopi

celery

karafs

cucumber

khiyär/bädrang

eggplant

bädemjän/ bänjän siyäh

green beans

lubiyä sabz

green pepper

felfel sabz/murche sabz

lettuce

kähu

okra

bämiye

mushroom

ghärch/samäragh

onion

piyäz

peas

nokhod

potato

sib zamini/kachälu

red beans

lubiyä ghermez/lubiyä surkh

spinach

esfenäj/pälak

tomatto

goje farangi/bänjän rumi

vegetables

sabzijät

FRUITS & NUTS

almond

bädäm

apple

sib

apricot

zard älu

banana

moz/kila

berry

tut

cherry

giläs

conconut

närgil

fig

anjir

grape

angur

grapefruit

gripfurut

hazelnut

fandogh

kiwifruit

kivi

lemon

limu

mandarin

närengi/mälta

melon

kharboze

nut

äjil/miwa khushk

orange

porteghäl/närenj

peach

hulu

pear

goläbi/näk

peanut

bädäm zamini

pineapple

änänäs

pistachio

peste

plum

älu

pomegrante

anär

strawberry

tut farangi/tut zamini

watermelon

hendväne/tarbuz

SPICES & CONDIMENTS

cinemon

därchin

fruit jam

morabbä

garlic

sir

lemon

limu

oil

roghan

olive oil

roghan e zeytun

onions

piyäz

red peppers

felfel e gharmez/ murch e surkh

saffron

za'ferän

salt

namak

suger

shekar/bura

turmeric

zard chube

vinegar

serke

DRINKS

boiled water

äb e jush

fruit juice

äb mive

coffee

ghahve/käfi

mineral water

äb ma'dani

soft drink

nushäbe

tap water

äb e shir/äb e tap

(cup of) tea

chäyi

with/without milk

bä/bedun e shir

with/without sugar

bä/bedun e shekar/bura

water

äb

yoghurt drink

dugh

IN THE COUNTRY

CAMPING

backpack

kule poshti

camping

chador zadan/khayma zadan

campsite

mahall e chädorz adan/ sähaye khay-ma zadan

can opener

dar bäzkon

compass

ghotbnamä

fire wood

hizom

hammer

chakkosh

mat

hasir

mattress

toshak

rope

tanäb/rismän

sleeping bag

kise khäb

stove

ojägh/däsh

tent

chador/khayma

tent peg

mikh e chador/ mikh e khayma

torch (flashlight)

cherägh ghovve/barghe dasti

water bottle

botri ye äb/botel e äb

Can we camp here?

mitavänim injä chador/khayma beza-nim?

Are there shower facilities?

injä dush/shäwer därad?

Can we make a fire here?

mitavänim injä ätish roshan konim?

Where's the electric hookup?

piriz/säket e bargh kojä hast?

Where's the shower/toilet?

dush/tuvälet/shäwer/tashnäb kojä hast

Where can I fill the gas cylinder

kojä mitavänam gäz rä por konam?

Who owns this land?

in zamin mäl e ki hast?

HIKING

Are there any tourist attractions here?

injä jähäye didani baräye turistä hast?

Where is the nearest village?

nazdiktarin rustä/gharya kojä hast?

Is it safe to climb this mountain?

bälä raftan az in kuh bikhatar hast?

Is there a hut up there?

panähgähi dar än bälä hast?

Do we need a guide?

rähnamä läzem därim?

I'd like to talk to a local guide.

mikhäham bä yek rähnamäye mahalli sohbat konam/gap bezanam

How long is the trail?

in safar cheghdr tul mikeshad?

Is the track well marked?

in masir khob alämat gozäri shode?

How high is the climb?

ertefä cheghadr hast?

Which is the shortest route?

kutähtarin räh kodäm hast?

Which is the easiest route?

äsäntarin räh kodäm hast?

Is the path open?

in masir bäz hast?

When does it get dark?

havä key tärik mishavad?

Where can we buy supplies?

az kojä mitavänim vasäyel/sämän bek-harim?

WEATHER

What's the weather like?

havä chetor hast?

Today it is ...

emruz havä ... hast

cloudy

abri

cold

sard/khonok

hot

dagh

warm

garm

windy

bädi/shamäli

It's raining heavily.

bärän/bärish e shadidi miyäyad

It's raining lightly.

bärän/bärish e kami miyäyad

It's flooding.

seyl miyäyad

autumn

päyiyz/khazän

to freeze

yakh zadan

ice

yakh

snow

barf

snowy

barfi

spring

bahär

storm

tufän

summer

täbestän

sun

aftäb

typhoon

gerdbäd

weather

havä

wind

bäd/shamäl

winter

zemestän

GEOGRAPHICAL TERMS

beach

sähel

bridge

pol

cave

ghär

cliff

sakhre

earthquake

zelzele

farm

mazre'e/f

footpath

radd e pä

forest

jangal

harbour

eskele

hill

tappe

hot spring

cheshme ye äb garm

house

khäne

island

jazire

lake

daryäche

mountain

kuh

peak

gholle

river

rudkhäne/daryä

sea

daryä/bahr

valley

darre

waterfall

äbshär

Sights

ancient

bästäni

church

kelisä

fortress

ghal'e

historical

tärikhi

mosque

masjed

museum

muze/miyuziyum

old

ghadimi

ruin

kharäbe

shrine

maghbare

statue

mojassame

FAUNA

Farm animals

calf

gusäle

camel

shotor

cat

gorbe/pishak

chicken

morgh

rooster

khurus

cow

gäv

dog

sag

donkey

olägh/khar

duck

ordak

goat

boz

goose

ghäz

horse

asb

sheep

gusfand

lamb

barre

WILDLIFE

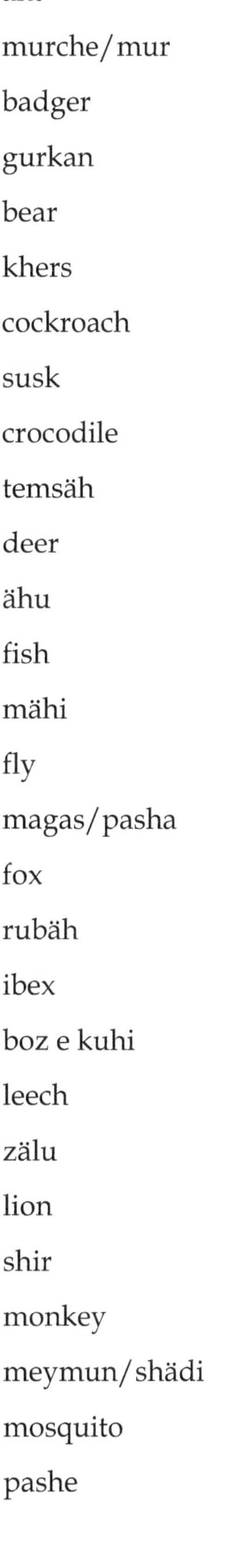

ant

murche/mur

badger

gurkan

bear

khers

cockroach

susk

crocodile

temsäh

deer

ähu

fish

mähi

fly

magas/pasha

fox

rubäh

ibex

boz e kuhi

leech

zälu

lion

shir

monkey

meymun/shädi

mosquito

pashe

pig

khuk

rabbit

khargush

snake

mär

spider

ankabut

tiger

babr

wolf

gorg

rhindeer

gavazn

BIRDS

bird

parande

butterfly

parväne

buzzard

läshkhor

crow

kalägh

eagle

oghäb

patridge

kabk

quail

belderchin

harrier

bäz

owl

jughd

sparrow

gonjeshk

stork

laklak

vulture

karkas

woodpecker

därkub

FlORA & AGRICULTURE

agriculture

keshävarzi/zirä'at

banana

moz/kila

barley

jo

corn

zorrat/jawäri

cotton

panbe

crops

mahsul/häsil

farmer

keshävarz/dehghän

flower

gol

grapes

angur

harvest (verb)

bardäsht/dero

irrigation

äbyäri

leaf

barg

planting/sowing

käshtan

rice field

shälizär

sunflower

äftäbgardän

sultana

keshmesh

tobacco

tanbäku

tree

derakht

wheat

gandom

HEALTH

AT THE DOCTOR

Where is the ...?

 ... kojä hast?

How do you feel?

häletän chetor hast?

doctor

doctor/däktar

hospital

bimärestän/shafäkhäna

chemist

därukhäne/daväkhäna

dentist

dandänpezeshk/däktar e dandän

I'm sick.

marizam/näkhosham

My friend is sick.

dustam mariz hast/dust am näkhosh hastI need a doctor who speaks Eng-

lish.

man doktore ingilisi zabän läzem däram

It hurts there.

änjä dard mikonad

I feel nauseous.

hälat e tahavvo' däram

I've been vomiting.

estefrägh mikonam

I feel better/worse.

häl am behtar/badtar hast

Can the doctor come here?

doktor mitavänad injä biyäyad?

I have caught a cold

sarmä khordam/rizesh kardam

What's the matter?

chi shode?

Do you feel any pain?

dard däri?

Where does it hurt?

kojä dard mikonad?

Are you menstruating?

periyod in?

Do you have a temperature?

tab däri?

How long have you been like this?

chand vaghte intor hasti?

Have you had this before?

ghablan intori shodi?

Are you on medication?

däru masraf mikoni/davä migiri?

Do you smoke?

sigär/segret mikeshi?

Do you drink?

mashrub mikhori?

Do you take drugs?

mavadde mokhadder masraf mikoni?

Are you allergic to anything?

be chizi hassasiyyat däri?

Are you pregnant?

hämele in?

I'm ill.

man marizam

I've been vomiting.

estefrägh mikonam

I have a burn on my (hand)

(dast) am sukhte

I have an infection on my (foot)

(pä) yam ufunat karde

I have a sprain in my (ankle)

man (moch e pä) yam pich khorde

I have a cough

man sorfe mikonam

I feel nauseous.

hälate tahavvo' däram

I can't sleep.

nemitavänam bekhäbam

I feel …

man ehsäs… däram

dizzy

sargije/sarcharkhi

shivery

larz

weak

za'if

I have …

man … däram

an allergy

hassäsiyyat

anaemia

kam khuni

a burn

sukhtegi

cancer

saratän

a cold

sarmä khordegi/rizesh

constipation

yubusat/ghabziyat

cystitis

kist

diarrhoea

eshäl

a fever

tab

gastroenteritis

eltehäb e me'de vo rude

a headache

sardard

a heart condition

närähati ye ghalbi

indigestion

su' e hazeme

a migraine

migrin

a pain

dard

a sore throat

galu dard

a stomackache

me'de dard

a toothache

dandän dard

a urinary infection

ufunat e majäri ye edrär

venereal disease

bimäri ye urughi

worms

kerm

I feel better/worse.

häl am behtar/badtar hast

I usually take this medicine.

ma'mulan in däru/davä rä mikkoram

I have been vaccinated.

väksan zadam/man vaksin gerefte am

I want a receipt for my insurance?

baräye bime am resid mikhäham

I have …

man … däram

diabet

diyäbet

asthm

äsmä

anaemia

kam khuni

I'm allergic to …

man be … hassäsiyyat däram

antibiotics

äntibiyutik

aspirin

äsperin

bees

zanbur

codeine

kode'in

dairy products

labaniyyät

penicillin

penisilin

pollen

garde

I have a skin allergy.

man ye hassasyyat e posti/jildi däram

I've had my vaccinations.

väksanhäm rä zadam/vaksinam rä gerefte am

I have my own syringe.

man khodam sorang/sirinj däram

I'm on medication for …

man baräye … däru/davä masraf mikonam

I need a new pair of glasses.

man ye eynak e täze lazem däram

addiction

e'tiyäd

bite (insect)

nish

bite (dog)

gäz

blood test

äzemäyesh e khun

contraceptive

zedd e hämelegi

injection

tazrigh/pichkäri

injury

jarähat

vitamins

vitämin

wound

zakhm

PARTS OF THE BODY

ankle

moch e pä/bajalak e pä

appendix

äpändis

arm

bäzu

back

posht

bladder

masäne

blood

khun

bone

ostukhän

chest

sine

ear

gush

eye

cheshm

finger

angosht

foot

pä

hand

dast

head

sar

heart

ghalb

kidney

koliye/gorda

knee

zänu

legs

sägh

liver

kabed/jigar

lungs

riye/shosh

mouth

dahan

muscle

azole

ribs

dande/ghabirgha

shoulder

shäne

skin

pust/jild

stomach

me'de

teeth

dandän

throat

galu

AT THE CHEMIST

I need some medicine for …

däruyi/daväyi baräye …mikhäham

Does this medicine need a prescrip-tion?

in däru/davä noskhe läzem därad?

How many times a day?

chand bär dar ruz?

Four times a day.

chahar bär dar ruz

Once every six hours

har shish sä'at yek bär

Are there side effects?

avärez e jänebi därad?

antibiotics

äntibiyutik

antiseptic

zedd e ufuni konande

bandage

bändäzh

cotton balls

panbe

cough medicine

däruye/daväye sorfe

laxatives

molayyen

painkillers

mosakken

rubbing alcohol

alkol

sleeping pills

ghors e khäb

AT THE DENTIST

I have a toothache.

man dandän am dard mikonad

I have a hole.

dandän am suräkh shode

I've broken my tooth.

dandän am shekaste

My gums hurt.

Lase/bira am dard mikonad

I don't want it extracted.

nemikhäham än rä bekishin

Ouch!

äkh

ON BUSSINESS

We're attending a ...

mä dar yek ... sherkat/ishtiräk mikonim

conference

konferäns

meeting

jalase

trade fair

namäyeshgäh e bäzargäni

I have an appointment with ...

man bä ... gharär däram

Here's my business card.

in kärt e bäzargäni ye man hast

I need an interpreter.

man yek motarjem/tarjumän lazem/zarurat däram

I need to use a computer.

man yek kämpiyuter läzem/zarurat däram

I need to send a fax/an email.

man mikhäham ye faks/imeyl beferestam/rawän konam

USEFUL WORDS

cellular/mobile phone

telfon e hamräh/mobäyl

client

arbäb ruju'

colleague

hamkär

distributor

tozi' konande

email

imeyl

exhibition

namäyeshgäh

manager

modir

profit

sud

proposal

tarh

ON TOUR

We're part of a group.

mä joz' e ye guruh/gurup hastim

We're tourists.

Mä jahängard/turist hastim

I'm with the ...

man bä … am

team

tim

Please speak with our manager.

lotfan bä modir e mä sohbat konin

We've lost our equipment.

mä vasäyel/sämän emän rä gom kardim

flight

parväz

train

ghatär/rail

PILGRIMAGE & RELIGION

What is your religion?

din e shomä chi hast?

I'm ...

man … am

Buddhist

budäyi

Christian

Masihi/isawi

Hindu

hendu

Jewish

yahudi/juhud

Muslim

mosalmän

I'm not religious.

man mazhabi nistam

I'm (Catholic).

man (kätolik) am.

I believe in God.

man be khodä mo'taghed am

I believe in destiny/fate.

man be sarnevesht mo'taghed am

I'm interested in astrology/philosophy.

be setäre shenäsi/falsafe aläghe däram

Can I pray here?

man mitavänam injä ebädat konam?

Where can I pray/worship?

man kojä mitavänam ebädat konam?

church

kelisä

god

khodä

prayer

do'ä/ebädat

priest

keshish

shrine

maghbare

TIME & DATES

What time is it?

sä'at chand hast/chand baja hast?

(It's) one o'clock.

sä'at yek hast/yak baja hast

(It's) ten o'clock.

sä'at dah hast/dah baja hast

Half past five

panj o nim

It's 14.15.

sä'at chähärdah o punzdah daghighe

It's 20 to 12.

 sä'at bist daghighe be daväzdah

The bus leaves at 5.10

 utubus/bas panj o dah daghighe harekat mikonad

The train should arrive at 18 minutes to six

ghatär bäyad hijdah daghighe be shish beresad

DAYS OF THE WEEK

The week starts at Saturday and ends in Friday. So, unlike in west, weekend days are Thurseday and Friday.

Monday

doshanbe

Tuesday

seshanbe

Wednesday

chähärshanbe

Thursday

panjshanbe

Friday

jom'e

Saturday

shanbe

Sunday

yekshanbe

MONTHS

January

zhänviye/janyuweri

February

fevriye/februweri

March

mars/märch

April

ävril/äpril

May

meh/mey

June

zhu'an/jun

July

zhu'iyye/julay

August

ut/ägest

September

septämr/september

October

oktobr/oktober

November

novämr/november

December

desämr/desember

Persian months are different from English.

Persian months   starts at:

farvardin   21 March-

ordibehesht 21 April

khordäd   22 May

tir   22 June

mordäd   23 July

shahrivar   23August

mehr   23 September

äbän   23 October

äzar   22 November

dey   22 December

bahman   21 January

esfand 20 February

SEASONS

summer

täbestän

autumn

päyiyz/khazän

winter

zemestän

spring

bahär

DATES

Because Persian calendar is completely different from Christian one, people cannot tell you the Christian date without looking to the calendar. All the official dates in Iran are in Persian calendar, which is solar and 364 days.

PRESENT

What day is today?

emruz che ruzi hast?

Today is Tuesday.

emruz seshanbe ast

today

emruz

this morning

emruz sob

tonight

emshab

this week

in hafte

this year

emsäl

now

hälä

early/late

zud/dir

this month

in mäh

every hour/day/month

har sä'at/ruz/mäh

PAST

six hours and 25 minutes before

shish sä'at o bis rä panj daghighe gha

nine hours afterwards

noh sä'at ba'd

yesterday

diruz

day before yesterday

pariruz

yesterday morning

diruz sob

last night

dishab

last week

hafte ye gozashte

last month

mäh e gozashte

last year

pärsäl

FUTURE

in 20 minutes

dar bist daghighe

three hours from now

se sä'at ba'd az in

How many hours does it take?

chand sä'at tul mikeshad?

It takes…hours.

…sä'at tul mikeshad

It takes…minutes.

…daghighe tul mikeshad

When will you come back.

shomä key bar migardin?

I'll stay for four days/weeks.

man chähär ruz/hafte mimänam

tomorrow

fardä

day after tomorrow

pas fardä

tomorrow morning

fardä sob

tomorrow afternoon

fardä ba'd az zohr/asr

tomorrow evening

fardä shab

next week/month

hafte/mäh e ba'd

next year

säl e ba'd

soon/right away

bezudi/foran

DURING THE DAY

afternoon

ba'd az zohr/asr

dawn

sahar

day

ruz

early

zud

midnight

nesf e shab

morning

sob

night

shab/shäm

noon

zohr

sunrise

tulu'

sunset

gurub

second (time)

säniye

sometimes

ba'zi maväghe'

fast/slow

tond/kond

FESTIVALS

Festive Expressions

happy new year

säl e no mobärak

happy your festivity

eyd e shomä mobärak

NUMBERS & AMOUNTS

The numbers in Persian are written in Arabic. Unlike the letters, numbers are
written from left to right.

CARDINAL NUMBERS

1	yek
2	do
3	se
4	chähär
5	panj
6	shish
7	haft
8	hasht
9	noh
10	dah
11	yäzdah
12	daväzdah
13	sizdah
14	chähärdah
15	punzdah
16	shunzdah
17	hifdah
18	hijdah
19	nuzdah
20	bist
21	bist rä yek
22	bist rä do
30	si
40	chehel

50	panjäh
60	se
70	haftäd
80	hashtäd
90	navad
100	sad
200	divist/dosad
300	sisad/sesad
400	chähärsad
500	pänsad/panjsad
600	shishsad
700	haftsad
800	hashtsad
900	nohsad
1000	hezär
2000	do hezär
2200	do hezär rä divist
45	chehel rä panj
167	sad rä se rä haft
1320	hezär rä sisad rä bist
1999	hezär rä nohsad rä navad rä noh
14800	chähärdah hezär rä hashtsad
one million	yek milyon

ORDINAL NUMBERS

1st	avval
2nd	dovvom
3rd	sevvom

6th	shishom
13th	sizdahom
20th	bistom
58th	panjäh rä hashtom
100th	sadom
188th	sad rä hashtäd rä hashtom

FRACTIONS

1/4	chärak/yek chähärom
1/3	sols/yek sevvom
1/2	nesf
3/4	se chähärom
none	hich

EMERGENCIES

Help!

komak!

Stop!

ist!

Go away!

gom sho!

Thief!

dozd!

Fire!

ätish!

Watch out!

moväzeb bäsh!

It's an emergency.

ezteräri hast

Could you help us please?

mitavänin lotfan be mä komak konin?

Could I please use the telephone?

lotfan mitavänam yek telefon bezana

I'm lost.

man gom shodam

Where is the toilet?

tuvälet kojä hast?

Call the police!

polis rä khabar konin!

Where is the police station?

edäre ye polis kojä hast?

bags

kif

handbag

kif dasti

money

pul

papers

madärek (madärek)

passport/gozarnäme

päsport

HEALTH

Call a doctor!

yek doktor khabar konin

Call an ambulance!

yek ämbuläns khabar konin

I am ill.

man mariz am

My friend is ill.

dust e man mariz hast

I have medical insurance.

man bime ye darmäni/tibbi däram

Could I use the telephone?

mitavänin yek telefon bezanam

Concluding page

Language is one of the strongest bonds that connect human beings. The Persian (Farsi & Dari) Phrasebook was created to help learners not only understand words but also communicate with empathy, curiosity, and respect across cultures.

Through its simple expressions, pronunciation guides, and clear grammar explanations, this book empowers readers to connect confidently with Persian speakers in Iran, Afghanistan, and beyond.

Learning a language is more than memorizing vocabulary — it is discovering another worldview. It allows us to listen, to appreciate differences, and to see the shared humanity that unites us all. May this phrasebook accompany you in travel, study, and friendship, and remind you that every word spoken with kindness shortens the distance between people.

About the Author

Dr. Dehghani has authored several dictionaries and language-learning books, including the Persian–English English–Persian Learner's Dictionary (Ibex Publishers, 2006). His teaching and writing are de-voted to making languages accessible, practical, and culturally meaningful. A passionate advocate of intercultural understanding, he continues to write and lecture on language, identity, and migration.

www.yadehghani.com